COTTAGE POETRY

COLETTA ROHAN

Ho'ohana

COPYRIGHT

Added reflections by Kevin and Michele Foley

ISBN: 979-8-9905814-1-8

Library of Congress Control Number: TX0004429664

Acknowledgement

This collection stands as a reflection of Mary Foley's faith, love, and gift for words. We honor the devotion of her husband, Daniel M. Foley, whose steadfast support gave her strength, and the inspiration she found daily in her children—Daniel Jr., Kathleen, Barbara, Carolyn, Ann, Joyce, Patrick, Kevin, and Michael. Their love, laughter, and even their shenanigans filled her life with richness that blossomed into poetry.

We remain grateful to the friends and family who encouraged her to share her gift, leading to the publication of her first book in 1996 and continuing to inspire this edition.

As a note for today's readers, The cover image of this book was generated entirely by artificial intelligence using ChatGPT, powered by OpenAI. This image is disclosed in accordance with Amazon KDP's AI content guidelines.

MY MOTHER - REFLECTIONS IN A MIRROR

♥

I turned around today
 and caught a glimpse
of someone once I knew.
The smile, the eyes reflected there
a bright and shining blue.
She rests beneath the blessed earth,
her spirit soaring free,
and yet I look again and see,
she still lives on in me.

♥

DESCRIBE MEMORIES OF YOUR MOTHER OR MATERNAL ROLE MODEL.

TRAVELING

♥

We fly along – my car and I.

The hills and valleys passing by.

The idle box cars dot the land.

Farms and cows, but where is Man?

DESCRIBE YOUR DREAM TRIP TO AN AREA WHERE YOU CAN SEE THE STARS.

ON FRIENDSHIP

♥

Why did you never speak,
     or even look my way?
Our eyes might meet and then,
yours quickly turn away.
Your friendly smile I've noticed when
the rich and famous pass your way.
Is it because my skin is brown and yours
is white, that makes your turn away?
Or tho' I'm white I do not fit into your
social whirl –
But when we stand before the lord and life has
quickly flown -------I'll look to you again and hope
We'll both be welcomed home

♥

WRITE THREE SENTENCES ABOUT A UNIQUE FRIENDSHIP YOU HAVE HAD.

BEACH TOWELS

♥

The beach towels hanging on the line
    bring thoughts of summers past.
The little ones around the pool
and playing on the grass.
They used to be afraid, but then
the water beckoned them.
And Daddy's arms held them tight, while learning how
to swim.
"Look at me," they'd cry, "see Grandma
I can swim." While Grandpa sits and watches
the joy his labors brought.
The towels I'll shake and fold and smooth,
and fondly put away,
'till summer comes around again
and Grandkids come to play.

♥

WHAT MEMORIES DO YOU HAVE OF GRANDPARENTS?

MOMENTS LOST

♥

I meant to stop and say hello Mom, but today was pretty busy.

A meeting here, a luncheon there, a trip into the city.

I know we planned to meet today, for lunch and then a show.

Maybe next week, things will be more slow.

My star is rising now you know, so I must play to win.

I know you'll understand Mom, I'll call when I have time again.

My Mom was laid to rest today and on her desk I see,

a date crossed out for lunch and show.

A special day with me.

I can't remember now at all, what I did that day.

My tears fall gently on the ground, I turn and walk away.

I've won my star, but lost my crown.

My Mom has passed away.

WHO DO YOU NEED TO SPEND TIME WITH AND WHY?

I LOVED YOU

♥

You never told me that you loved me,
but I saw it in your eyes.
So shy and yet so loving,
but we had to compromise.
I told you that I loved you
and really knew you cared,
as side by side, we walked through life,
and older day by day...
You finally said "I love you,"
and then life slipped away.
But dear God he said "I loved you".
The sweetest words, this side of heaven,
I'd always longed to hear.

♥

WHO DO YOU KNOW THAT NEEDS TO HEAR, "I LOVE YOU."

ONLY LOGIC WILL PREVAIL

♥

He looks in hopeless wonder – at a
father who cannot see –
His dreams – his hopes – excitement,
over life and what it could be.
(only logic will prevail)
No "well done son," "yes try it"
(Only logic will prevail)
"it can't be done, don't try it" – he
turns away again.
Is one right, is one wrong?
No, just the difference, between two men.
A father and son.

♥

DESCRIBE A TIME WHEN YOU LONGED TO HEAR WORDS OF ENCOURAGEMENT.

ON DYING

D ear Lord -----when I die
      will You be there?
To hold my hand to show You care?
And will I weep for those I love?
Quiet tears of love.
To leave them here -----
to see Your face ----
To rest in peace.

WHAT IS ON YOUR BUCKETLIST?

REMEMBER ME?

♥

On "the way up," you passed me by.
    We used to be friends.
I wondered why – you didn't call,
or have the time to spend, with me again.
How sad for me was your ascent,
and though I'm glad to see,
"you have arrived."
The price to pay for me was high,
A friendship cast aside.

WHAT FRIENDSHIP WOULD YOU LIKE TO RENEW?

YOU WANT ME LORD?

♥

You want me Lord?

But why?

I'm not ready yet.

I have so much to do.

Are you sure it is me you're calling Lord?

I feel so young and spry.

There's a bit of gray on top ----

and wrinkles 'round the eye

But surely Lord you can't believe, I'm ready yet to die.

I know to them I'm "old,"

Was it only yesterday – that I was young as they?

Okay, I'm ready Lord.

I guess You know what's best.

I'll put my hand in Yours dear Lord, and seek Eternal rest.

♥

WHAT DO YOU NEED TO FINISH BEFORE GOD CALLS YOU?

SEASONS

♥

Where I live the leaves don't change
to many shades and hues.
When winter comes the trees still bloom,
and yet we too can see – that nature
lets us know – in many subtle ways ---
the shortening of the days.
Long evenings that we all enjoyed,
have slowly slipped away,
and darkness brings us all inside,
at closing of the day.

WHAT DO YOU LOVE ABOUT YOUR FAVORITE SEASON?

TOMORROW

♥

My old friends are gone,
        now their houses too –
demolished today by a wrecking crew.
The trees they planted when they were young,
standing bleakly in the noon day sun
as if to say "please take me too."
But tomorrow comes, and in their place,
will come some new and shining face.
A home will grow and children too,
and life will then begin anew.
I feel the tears fall slowly now,
they wet my cheeks and I recall
those friends who helped when I was young.
I'll do the same for those to come.

♥

WHO HELPED YOU WHENEVER YOU MOVED INTO A NEW PLACE?

THE LAST ROSE

♥

The leaves are falling all around
the sky is steely gray.
The north wind blows and numbs my toes
but look what I have found!
One last rose still blooming there,
it's colors bright and true.
My spirit lifts,
my heart's delight.
I'll bring that rose to you!

♥

HOW DO YOU FEEL WHEN SUMMER ENDS, THE WEATHER COOLS, AND THE FLOWERS HIBERNATE?

A GRANDCHILD'S LOVE

♥

Y ou accept me as I am little man -----
     No questions asked, just hugs and kisses,
or "come play with me Grandma."
I haven't accomplished much they say ---
always there though, to talk and listen
when someone calls.
And you little one – little girl ---
full of giggles
"Come sit Grandma and read a story," you say.
Your love is what I need today!

RECALL A PRECIOUS MOMENT WITH A CHILD, WRITE ABOUT HOW IT MADE YOU FEEL.

OH PRIEST

♥

When I was a child
    You told me to "believe"
and I believed.
When you held the "Host" up high
So high I thought it would touch the sky –
and said "this is the Christ"
I believed.
But now I'm grown –
and as I sit and watch –
I wonder,
"Oh Priest, do you believe?"

♥

HOW DID YOU FEEL WHEN YOU REALIZED YOUR RELIGIOUS LEADER HAD FLAWS?

SUMMER RAIN

A soft breeze – brings the scent
of summer rain.
My mind returns to warm summer days –
splashing through puddles –
my brothers and I.
Faces upturned and arms outstretched
we run along –
the warm drops against our sun bronzed skin.
I see a young girl – spindly and long –
Hair plastered to her face –
delighting in this mid-summer's song.
Then I return to my tasks
and once again store –
those memories away –
perhaps to be resurrected once more –
by the sweet scent of rain
on a soft summer day.

♥

DESCRIBE THE LAST TIME YOU PLAYED IN THE RAIN LIKE A CHILD.

COMPANY'S COMIN'

D oin' the dishes, Moppin' the floor
     Answerin' the phone, Knock on the door.
  Makin' the beds, Rakin' the yard
  Buyin' some food, Working so hard.
  Stoppin' to rest, Then dressin' up
  'cause "Company's Comin" and must look my best.
  Time is a flyin', Knock on the door
  Eyes start to sparkle, laughter begins.
  Workin' is over, day is all gone
  Guests have all left I'll sleep until dawn.
  Oh, baby is cryin' and dawn's far away
  We rock while I'm dreamin' of lands far away.

HOW DO YOU PREPARE FOR GUESTS?

AFTER FORTY YEARS

♥

We lie together he and I
       I move into the curve of his body,
until no space is in between.
It is early morning,
and we are still
only half awake.
We both lie curved in the fetal position,
my buttocks fitting into the curve of
his loins.
His arm curves under and around my neck,
his hand resting
on my breasts.
We lie and wait for dawn
wondering
who'll get up and put the coffee on?

♥

WRITE A SHORT POEM ABOUT THE ONE YOU LOVE.

POETS

A re all Poets dreamers?
        Or all dreamers Poets?
Seeing in their dreams
What we cannot see?
Or in their visions
what could be.
Are they inventors?
Mystics?
Sometimes scorned, for things
others cannot understand?
Derided – mocked
and sometimes shunned –
they weep at beauty –
are touched by lovers –
pained when others hurt.
A Poet is so many things –
that maybe only God can see –
and understand – a Poet.

WRITE A SHORT POEM ABOUT YOUR JOB.

LET THEM SING

♥

W hy do we have to die?

    I'd like to stay around

'stead of layin' underground

I'd hear the people walkin' round

and standing on the sod, talkin'

'bout this and that, and hushing

children, - - - - "for this is sacred ground

and she is close to God."

Let them run and play and sing

for I can hear them here,

and only wish I'd listened more,

to voices young and clear –

above the sod.

WHAT ARE SOME OF YOUR FAVORITE SONGS. WHY ARE THEY YOUR FAVORITES?

SPRING

♥

On top of a hill sits a tree
    and in the tree sits a bee,
looking for nectar
waiting for Spring -----
Oh little bee, like me!

WHAT DOES SPRING MEAN TO YOU?

ODE TO A MODERN OFFICE BUILDING

♥

I see you standing silent,
  Windows sparkling in the sunlight.
Story after story of windows,
but not a soul in sight.
Are people looking out as they work?
Do they see my car idling there –
at the red light?
I cannot see in.
As I look up, I wonder who they are.
A smile, a wave, might be nice.
Are they happy there –
In your prison of tinted glass?

♥

Write about the personalities of the buildings you drive by.

WAS I EVER TEN?

♥

Was I ever ten –
  Was I ever there?
Skipping rope –
Playing jacks –
It seems so long ago.
Was I ever ten –
I don't know.
Ridin' bikes –
Catchin' frogs –
Playing in the snow.
Was I ever ten?

WRITE A SHORT POEM ABOUT WHEN YOU WERE TEN.

POPPIES

T hank you God for Spring
    the flowers, the sun, the rain.
Thank you God for Spring
the poppies in the lane
flaming orange and yellow,
they dazzle all who see
Thank you God for Spring,
It means a lot to me.

DESCRIBE WHAT YOUR FAVORITE FLOWER LOOKS LIKE WHEN IT BLOOMS.

DEATH

♥

Death is but a dream away,
He's waiting for the morn'
He's standing waiting in the wings,
the moment you are born.
And all the years that go between,
are just a step towards fate.
He's standing waiting in the wings,
He only knows the date.

♥

WHAT WAS THE POET THINKING WHEN SHE WROTE THIS POEM?

MY HANDS – YOUR HANDS

D ear God these hands are Yours and mine.

You gave them to me to work for You.

They are showing signs of age, veins protruding, age spots ----

Grandma Hands my little Granddaughter says.

They have scrubbed and swept, cleaned and ironed –

cooked ten thousand meals or more –

(and sometimes got burned).

They have held a newborn son or daughter, nine in all,

and welcomed them with open arms, and Hands.

Patted little backs 'til that burp came up.

Wiped little bottoms and little runny noses.

Cleaned up vomit and wiped fevered brows. Bandaged cuts, then

held them while they cried, ('til it was all better).

Wiped away the tears of a daughter who had lost an infant son,

the tears of a daughter who had lost a husband.

Caressed a husband with love.

Held out these Hands to welcome a son away too long!

Held a hymnal to sing Your praises.

Helped a grandchild plant some seeds,

planted bulbs and flowers and even trees.

Raked and spaded, all of these – with these Hands.

Thank you Lord they still are strong,

You've blessed these Hands, You gave to me!

DESCRIBE WHAT YOUR HANDS HAVE DONE OVER THE YEARS.

A NOTE OF THANKS

♥

Thank you for spending time with *Cottage Poetry*. These poems are more than words on a page—they carry with them the spirit of my mother-in-law, Mary Foley, whose love of poetry lives on through these verses. Bringing her works to life has been both a privilege and a joy, and I hope that as you read, you felt some of the same light and comfort she gave to those around her.

My wish is that these verses not only brought a smile to your face, but also stirred memories of your own—moments of laughter, closeness, and love with family and friends. Poetry has a way of helping us pause, reflect, and reconnect with what matters most.